Acquisition & editorial:
  Nathaniel Gunod

Editor:
  Michael Rodman

Cover, cover photo, CD & interior design:
  Timothy Phelps

Music typesetting:
  Gary Tomassetti

CD recorded and engineered by
  Bar None Studio, Northford, CT

Book: ISBN 1-929395-45-0
Book and CD: ISBN 1-929395-46-9

Table of Contents

Introduction

Learning from the styles of the masters has always been central to music pedagogy. For years, these styles were drawn almost wholly from European classical traditions. When jazz, blues and rock began to be incorporated into music education, it was often as a "dessert," a departure from more "serious" studies. More recently, however, these styles have commanded new attention and respect in the world of pedagogy. The challenge now is to find educational materials that do justice to these styles and are compatible with traditional, classically based teaching methods.

The goal of the *Portraits* series is to provide exciting and stimulating pieces for keyboard students while inviting them to explore the traditions and great artists of jazz, blues and rock. Unlike many student-level pieces of a popular nature, the "portrait" format allows the student to associate the music he or she is playing with an actual artist. It is clear that a student's motivation increases greatly when he or she associates an assigned piece with real music—music by influential, well-known personalities who are amply represented on recordings. This can enhance the student's sense of pride and set the stage for learning about other great artists in any style. The personalities presented in the *Portraits* series are not meant to represent the "best" or "most important"; rather, each is simply part of a diverse cast of great artists. These artists cover a wide spectrum of styles and time periods, and each has left a rich legacy for musicians and music lovers.

Teachers and self-directed students using the *Portraits* series need not be experts in these styles. While these books are rooted in traditional piano pedagogy, the pieces themselves remain true to the styles that inspired them. They can be used as technical studies, recital pieces or repertoire for just jamming out. Teachers can be comfortable knowing that in studying these pieces, students will receive reinforcement in reading, rhythm, fingering, phrasing and other important areas. Students need only enjoy themselves as they explore some wonderful styles and artists. The bottom line is that the music is both educational *and* fun.

The pieces in this second *Portraits* book are arranged progressively, beginning with some that use fairly simple eighth note rhythms and basic chords and arpeggios. By the end of the book, the pieces incorporate elements like syncopation, triplets, sixteenth notes, greater rhythmic independence between the hands and a greater variety of chord inversions.

Enjoy!

About the Author

Born and raised in New Haven, Connecticut, Noah Baerman began piano studies at age eight. He received his first formal jazz training at the Educational Center for the Arts in New Haven and at Jackie McLean's Artists' Collective in Hartford. There, he began his professional jazz career, including a long and continuing association with saxophonist and fellow student Jimmy Greene; he also performed for fun with several rock bands. Noah went on to earn bachelor's and master's degrees in jazz studies from the Mason Gross School of the Arts at Rutgers University, and also taught several jazz courses there. While at Rutgers, he spent six years under the tutelage of the renowned jazz pianist Kenny Barron. Noah has worked in and around New York with a wide variety of artists, and from 1994 to 1999 he performed and recorded with the jazz quartet Positive Rhythmic Force (PRF).

Noah has also been active in interdisciplinary arts, creating pieces that employ spoken poetry, modern dance, theater and the visual arts. His performance time is spent freelancing throughout the East Coast as an organist and pianist, leading his jazz trio and serving as musical director for the soul group Mr. B's Boogie Band. He is also active as an educator and composer. Noah's other books include *Jazz Keyboard Harmony* and the three-volume *Complete Jazz Keyboard Method*, published by the Alfred Publishing Company, Inc., in conjunction with the National Keyboard Workshop, Inc. He lives in Connecticut with his wife, Kate TenEyck.

Acknowledgments

Thanks to all of my students; to Nat Gunod for his support of this project; to Tim, Gary, Dave, Michael, Paula and everyone else at NGW and Workshop Arts; to everyone at Alfred Publishing Company; to Collin Tilton at Bar None Studio; to Kenny Barron, Ted Dunbar, George Raccio, Ralph Bowen, Joyce Baxter, Nan DeLucia, Franya Berkman, Julie Strand, Dawn Revett, Emily Wilson, Jimmy Greene, Jason Berg, Sunny Jain, Ben Tedoff, Amanda Monaco, Bob Hart, Lea Osborne, Phil Schaap, Lewis Porter, Clara Shen, Wanda Maximilien and Eva Perriou-Varga; to the fine folks at the Rutgers Music Department, the Artists' Collective, ECA, The Country School, Oddfellows Playhouse, Wesleyan University's Center For the Arts, the Institute of Jazz Studies, It's Only Natural and the Middlesex Fruitery; to the TenEyck and Baerman familes; to Peter; to Kate, my everything; and to all the artists profiled in this book for the inspiration and for giving such great music to the world.

Suggestions for Using This Book

BIO PAGES

At the beginning of each piece is a page with a photo and brief biography of the artist who inspired it. Reading through the biography will help give you a feel for the artist's musical style. However, there is no better way to get in tune with an artist's style than to hear him or her in action, so listening to at least some of the selections in the "Essential Listening" lists is strongly encouraged. All albums cited were in print on CD at press time.

EXERCISES

Experience has shown that these pieces are learned much more effectively when preceded by preparatory exercises. In most cases, the exercises pinpoint some of the more challenging elements in the pieces, whether technical, rhythmic or stylistic. The exercises are designed to be repeated as many times as necessary.

FLEXIBILITY

Fingering, dynamics, pedaling and other such elements are marked in the music. If you are so inclined, feel free to experiment; try modifying these elements or shifting registers. In all cases, let the sonic result be your guide in deciding which changes are effective.

"SWING" EIGHTH NOTES

In most of these pieces, eighth notes are played in the traditional way. In some cases (*Mistress of Scat, Delivering the Message, Red-Hot Rag*), reference is made to "swing feel." While swing feel is ideally acquired through extensive study and exposure, it can be respectably simulated by using long-short pairs, in which the first note in an eighth-note pair is held for slightly longer than its normal value, while the second note is delayed and shortened accordingly. Another approach is to play them as though they were eighth-note triplets, with the first two eighths tied together. Whenever swing feel is called for, it also applies to eighth rests and dotted quarter notes, and should be used throughout the piece.

Swing eighths

CD

The optional CD for this book is meant to be used to reinforce the written music. It can be especially useful in clarifying and helping the player understand the stylistic and rhythmic subtleties unique to a style and used in an exercise or piece.

This symbol indicates the number of the CD track that corresponds with a given exercise. Track 1 includes a tuning note (A), so that electronic keyboards can be tuned to the CD.

Each piece in the book is presented in three versions on the CD. The first version is for piano alone; the second version is for piano and full band; and the third version is for band alone. This last option, which allows you to play along with the band, is one of the most important features of the CD. In addition to being fun, playing along with the music and hearing the rhythmic nuances and how the keyboard fits into the overall texture will add a level of understanding that is likely to carry over even when you play the piece as a solo.

This symbol indicates the numbers of the CD tracks that correspond with the three versions of each piece as listed above.

Improvisation Suggestions

> The pieces in *Portraits* may be played successfully as notated. The pieces may also serve as a basis for improvisation, and this page offers a few suggestions for those who want to improvise. This page is for you if:
>
> - You (or your teacher) have experience with improvisation in jazz/blues/popular styles.
> - You can play blues, major and minor scales in several keys.
> - You can identify chords in several keys and play them as both block chords and arpeggios.
> - You can play bass notes or chords in the left hand while soloing in the right hand.

If you decide to proceed with this page, use these suggestions as a point of departure and work according to your own improvisational skills and imagination. If you intend to use the pieces for a performance that includes improvisation, put some thought into the form. In most cases, you will need to insert a solo section, probably after having played the piece through, followed by a repeat of some or all of the written music.

SLIDING HOME

In this tune, the bass line (beginning in measure 9 on page 8, and again in measure 21 on page 9) delineates a 12-bar blues in D. Look at the chords that are outlined and/or implied by the bass line, then work on soloing over these chords using the D Blues scale, chord tones or a combination of these. The left hand can play either the chords or the bass line.

THUMPIN'

There are two sections in this tune that can be used as a basis for improvisation. The introduction is followed by a funky bass ostinato (beginning in measure 9 on page 24, and again in measure 25 on page 25). In these places, use the right hand to improvise over the left-hand bass line. For the series of two-handed stop-time phrases followed by lines for the right hand alone at the top of page 25, play the arpeggios at the beginning of each two-measure phrase, and solo in place of the right hand lines. Throughout, use the G Blues scale.

DELIVERING THE MESSAGE

This tune is in an AABA form comprised of eight-measure sections. You can solo either over the entire form, or in just the A or B section. For the A sections, vamp on an F chord in the left hand and use the F Blues scale to improvise in the right. Use the simplicity of this tune as an opportunity to reinforce the form, making sure to maintain eight-measure phrasing throughout. For the bridge (measures 17–24 on page 29), identify the chords in the I-IV-II-V progression. Use the F Blues scale, chord tones or a combination of these to create a right-hand solo; the left hand can play the roots or voice the chords. Be sure to maintain a swing feel throughout.

SHADES OF BLUE

Use measures 5–16 on page 36 as a starting point for improvisation. Here, the left hand lays out a 12-bar blues in C. Analyze and identify these chords, then play them in the left hand as the right hand solos with the C Blues scale, chord tones or a combination of these. *Shades of Blue* also provides a great opportunity for using different chord inversions in the left hand. Make sure to use swing eighths throughout.

RED-HOT RAG

Measures 5–16 on page 44 imply a 12-bar blues in C, while measures 53–64 on page 47 imply a 12-bar blues in D. Either or both of these can be used for soloing. For improvising in these sections, use the C and D Blues Scales, respectively, chord tones or a combination of these. The left hand can lay down chords for a basic 12-bar blues, or you can analyze the implied chords. You can keep the left-hand rhythms simple, play the left-hand part as written or even develop your own stride pattern like the one found in the piece. Make sure that *Red-Hot Rag* swings throughout.

Portrait:

Sliding Home

Few pop stars can claim to have musical roots as deep as those of **Bonnie Raitt**. Even when performing pop songs, Raitt retains the emotional depth of the blues and the intimacy of folk. Her stunning slide guitar skills are matched by few guitarists. She has also worked tirelessly as a social activist for causes ranging from the environment to financial aid for musicians left poor by unfair record contracts.

Raitt's father, John, was a well-known and successful Broadway performer. In the late 1960s, Raitt moved from Los Angeles to Boston and began performing with and learning from then-recently "rediscovered" blues giants like Mississippi Fred McDowell and Sippie Wallace. Raitt made her recording debut in 1971 with the album "Bonnie Raitt" and continued to release albums throughout the 1970s and 1980s. Though she was much admired, none of these records was a commercial success. That changed in 1989 with Raitt's comeback album, "Nick of Time." After a year on the charts, it became a number-one hit and won many awards, making Raitt a star at the age of 40. She enjoyed similar success with her next two albums, "Luck of the Draw" (1991) and "Longing in Their Hearts" (1994). Her newfound fame allowed her not only to reach a larger audience with her own music, but also to bring attention to some of the blues and R&B legends who had inspired her.

ESSENTIAL LISTENING:

Top Pick: "Give It Up" (1972)
Raitt's second album shows off the distinctive mixture of blues, folk and pop that is central to her style. Carefully chosen cover tunes take a place alongside Raitt originals like the title track and *You Told Me Baby*.

"The Bonnie Raitt Collection" (compilation; 1990)
This diverse collection draws from Raitt's Warner Brothers recordings of the 1970s and 1980s.

"Luck of the Draw" (1991)
"Luck of the Draw" cemented Raitt's star status, which is, as the album testifies, wholly deserved. Every song, including hits like *I Can't Make You Love Me* and *Something to Talk About,* is a winner.

"Fundamental" (1998)
Raitt took a raw and edgy turn with this recording while remaining true to her proven combination of great songs, terrific singing and killer slide guitar.

Bonnie Raitt *(Born 1949)*

EXERCISES

Sliding Home is a medium-tempo song. After a mellow eight-measure introduction, it changes key from C to D and continues in a rocking blues style, providing a taste of Raitt's musical world, where ballads and blues coexist. *Sliding Home* also touches on the types of phrases Raitt uses when playing *slide guitar* (which calls for a glass or metal cylinder that allows the player to "swoop" to or from a note). Because this effect isn't possible on the piano, *grace notes* (rapidly played decorative notes, notated smaller than usual, which come just before a main note/beat) are used to approximate the slide-guitar sound.

For Example 1, begin by learning the hands separately. The left hand plays a solid, repeated bass line, while the right hand focuses on a rising *minor 6th* (the interval from F♯ to D, or four whole steps). This figure is decorated with the pitches immediately adjacent to F♯ (G and F♮, as in the first measure below).

Example 2 includes a number of grace notes. Remember to treat these as decorations of the main note (in this case, B). Work to glide quickly through the grace notes and to keep the rhythm steady.

Example 3 includes more grace notes, which should be played as explained in the previous example. Notice that the first two measures are in *stop time*. This is a device often used in blues in which the rhythm section (here represented by the left hand) plays only on the downbeat, leaving it to the melody (in this case, the right hand) to fill in the remainder of the measure in an interesting, rhythmic way.

Sliding Home

for Bonnie Raitt

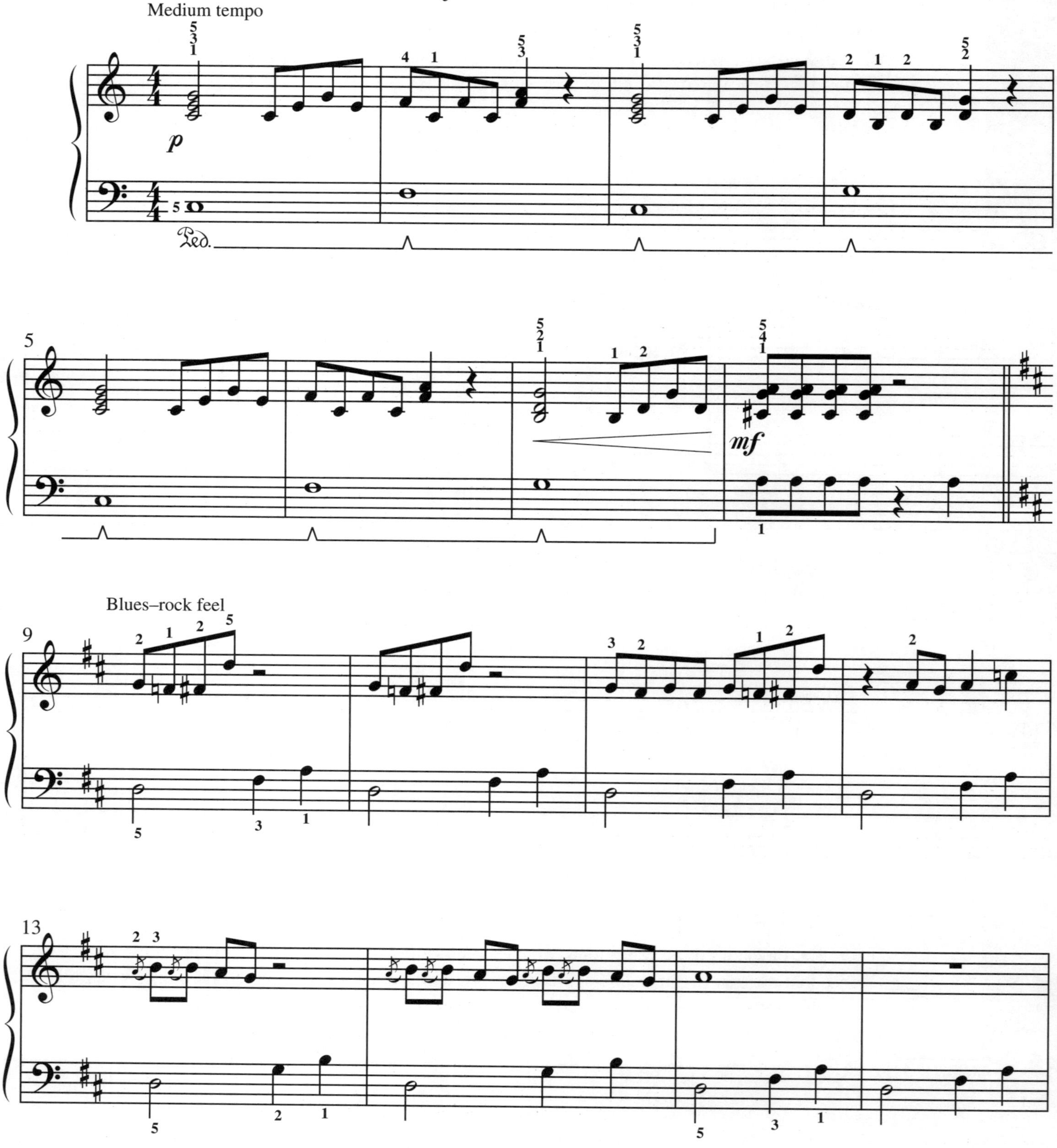

Pianist **Ahmad Jamal**'s career has been as unique as his influential playing style. While most jazz musicians first see fame recording and playing as sidemen (members of someone else's band), Jamal's first recorded success came with his own trio. His playing is famous for its economy; he never plays more than is called for. His music is full of passages that are sparse and colorful, but when technically challenging piano acrobatics are in order, he executes them with equal perfection. His trios (he has led several) are among the most interactive groups in jazz history.

After a stint with George Hudson's Orchestra in the late 1940s, Jamal formed his own piano-bass-guitar trio in the early 1950s. Among those influenced by this trio was legendary trumpet player and bandleader Miles Davis, who for years insisted that his pianists (notably Red Garland) emulate Jamal's style. By the late 1950s, Jamal had established his most famous trio, which included bassist Israel Crosby and drummer Vernell Fournier. The trio's live 1958 album, "At the Pershing: But Not For Me," remained a Top 40 pop hit for two years. Around this time, Ahmad opened his own nightclub, the Alhambra. Since then, his style has continued to evolve, his unique senses of musical taste and touch remaining intact.

ESSENTIAL LISTENING:

Top Pick: "At the Pershing: But Not For Me" (1958)
Elegant and swinging, this is the hit album (recorded live in Chicago) for which Jamal is best known. Jamal and company deftly swing through tunes like *Woody 'N' You* and *No Greater Love.*

"Poinciana" (1955)
The Portrait album "Poinciana" (not to be confused with the live Chess album of the same name), which includes tunes like *Ahmad's Blues*, features Ahmad's early, influential trio without drums (including guitarist Ray Crawford).

"Awakening" (1970)
This album of startlingly fresh trio music features Jamal, bassist Jamil Nasser and drummer Frank Gant. Jamal's touch and swing are in abundance in a gorgeous, sometimes ethereal, sometimes driving, very modern context.

"The Essence of Ahmad Jamal, Part 1" (1994)
The still-swinging Jamal put out this album in his 60s; saxophonist George Coleman is also featured. The diverse styles from different periods of Jamal's career here meld in a brilliant unified sound.

Ahmad Jamal *(born 1930)*

EXERCISES

On the album "But Not for Me," Ahmad Jamal performed a now-classic version of *Poinciana* in which he played sustained chords and short melodic passages on top of an infectious beat. This often-imitated beat, which became associated with Jamal and *Poinciana*'s drummer, Vernell Fournier, is also used in the laid-back *Alhambra*.

Begin by practicing Example 4 until the notes are accurate and the hands are well coordinated. Once this is accomplished, work on moving smoothly from one chord to the next. The pedal can be useful here, but it is not absolutely necessary; try playing the exercise both with and without the pedal, and compare the results. When you do use the pedal, take care not to let the chords overlap and get muddy. Experiment with the dynamics, too; try crescendos, diminuendos or even a combination of these (for example, begin at one volume, swell to another and then go back to where you began).

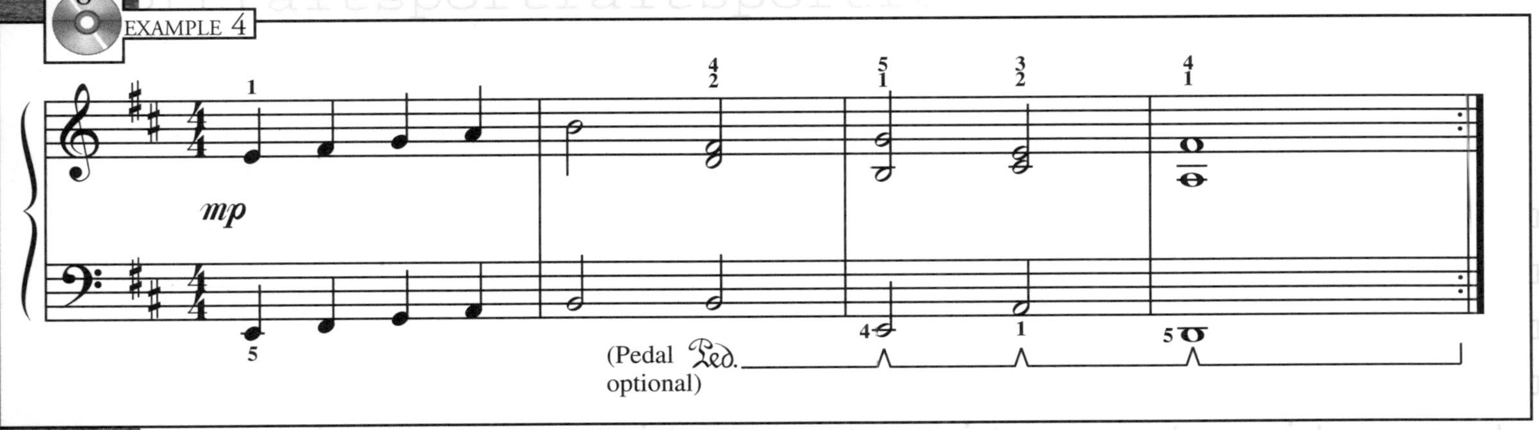

As in Example 4, begin by mastering the notes, then try playing both with and without the pedal. Strive to make the transitions from one chord to the next as smooth as possible.

Example 6 focuses on single-note interplay between the two hands, which recalls the back-and-forth of the players in some of Jamal's trios.

Alhambra
for Ahmad Jamal

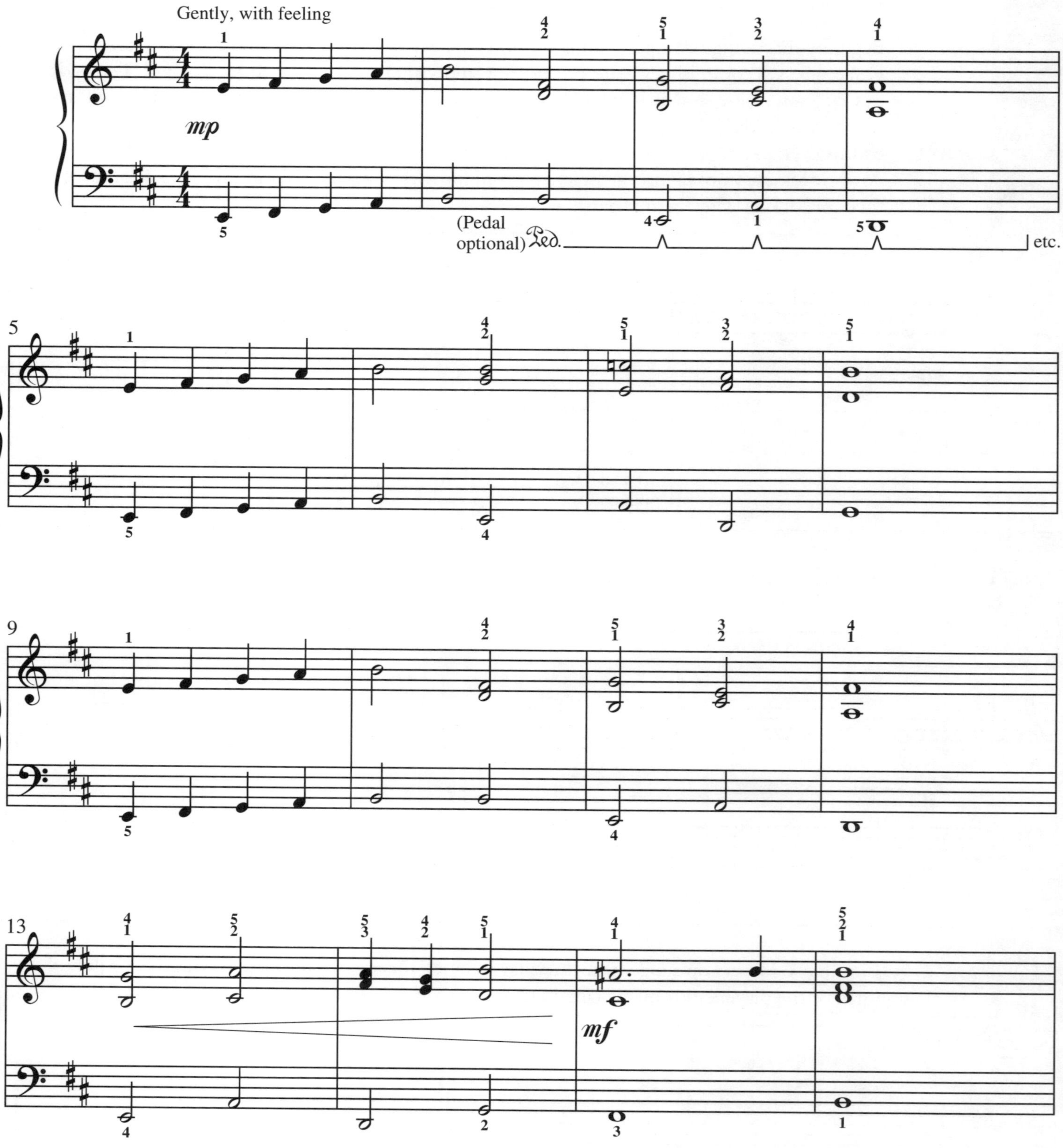

17
21
f
25
mp
29

If you've only heard of a single figure in *reggae* (a style that combines native Jamaican music with rock, soul and other popular influences), chances are good that it's **Bob Marley.** Marley was truly a giant—not just in the world of reggae, but in his international impact on popular music and his status as a cultural and political icon. Unquestionably the best-known reggae artist both inside and outside of Jamaica (the birthplace of the style), Marley was hugely influential and admired for his brilliant music, profound lyrics and impassioned singing.

In the early 1960s, Marley began making records in Jamaica and soon formed the Wailers, which included singer-songwriters Peter Tosh and Bunny Livingstone (better known as Bunny Wailer). In 1972, after years of struggle, the Wailers began making waves as recording artists with the international release of the album "Catch a Fire." The Wailers' recognition in the USA and Britain soared when Eric Clapton had a massive hit with Marley's song *I Shot the Sheriff* in 1974. Livingstone and Tosh left for solo careers in the mid-1970s, and the band continued as Bob Marley and the Wailers, featuring the I-Threes, a female vocal trio that included Marley's wife, Rita. Marley's success continued to grow until he died from cancer in 1980. Several of his children, most notably son David "Ziggy" Marley, have gone on to successful musical careers.

ESSENTIAL LISTENING:

Top Pick: "Legend" (compilation; 1984)
> This well-chosen collection is a great place to begin exploring Marley's music, though you won't want to stop here. All stages of Marley's career, from early classics like *Stir It Up* to brilliant later works like *Could You Be Loved,* are represented.

"Burnin'" (1973)
> This album helped to establish Marley and the Wailers outside Jamaica. The songs, playing and singing are all very powerful, ranging in mood from the bleakness of *Burnin' and Lootin'* to the optimism of *Hallelujah Time.*

"Live" (1975)
> "Live" does an excellent job of capturing the Wailers' power and intensity in live performance. These versions of *Get Up, Stand Up* and *No Woman, No Cry* are classics.

"Kaya" (1978)
> Though this mellow recording contains more love songs and fewer political songs than the Wailers' earlier albums, the music (including *Is This Love* and *Satisfy My Soul*) remains top-notch.

Bob Marley *(1945–1981)*

EXERCISES

Most reggae songs, including Bob Marley's, feature rhythms played on the weak beats (in $\frac{4}{4}$, beats 2 and 4), usually by the guitar and keyboard. *Rasta Prophet* is no different. Once you get used to the feeling of playing chords on these beats while maintaining the rhythmic flow, this song will feel totally natural.

The left-hand bass line in Example 7 should be solid but not stiff. When you work on the right hand, make sure that you are comfortable with the rhythm and that you can move from one chord to the next smoothly and without slowing down. Start slowly when you put the hands together, and take your time to make sure that the parts are well coordinated and that the reggae rhythm feels natural.

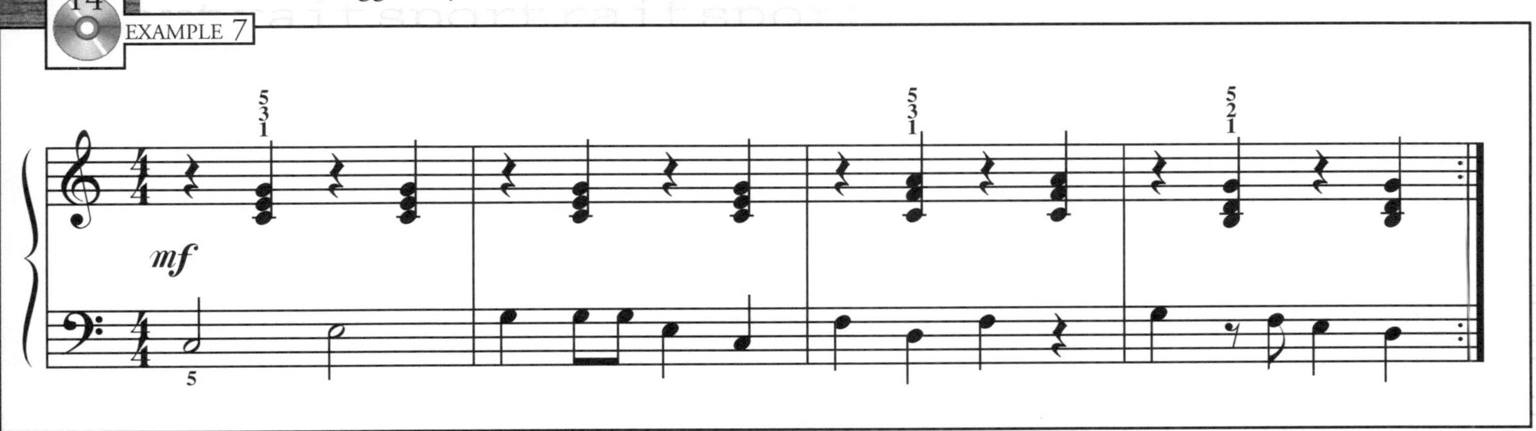

The *riff* (short, repeated passage) in Example 8 is used as a transition in the song. Note that the left-hand and right-hand parts are the same. Count it like this (playing on the italicized counts): *one and* two *and* three *four*. Make sure that your fingering is secure so that you can play this passage cleanly.

In Example 9, the right hand plays a more standard melody, while the left hand plays on both strong and weak beats. Make sure that the left hand is solid before adding the right and that you can play the rhythms accurately and with a laid-back feeling.

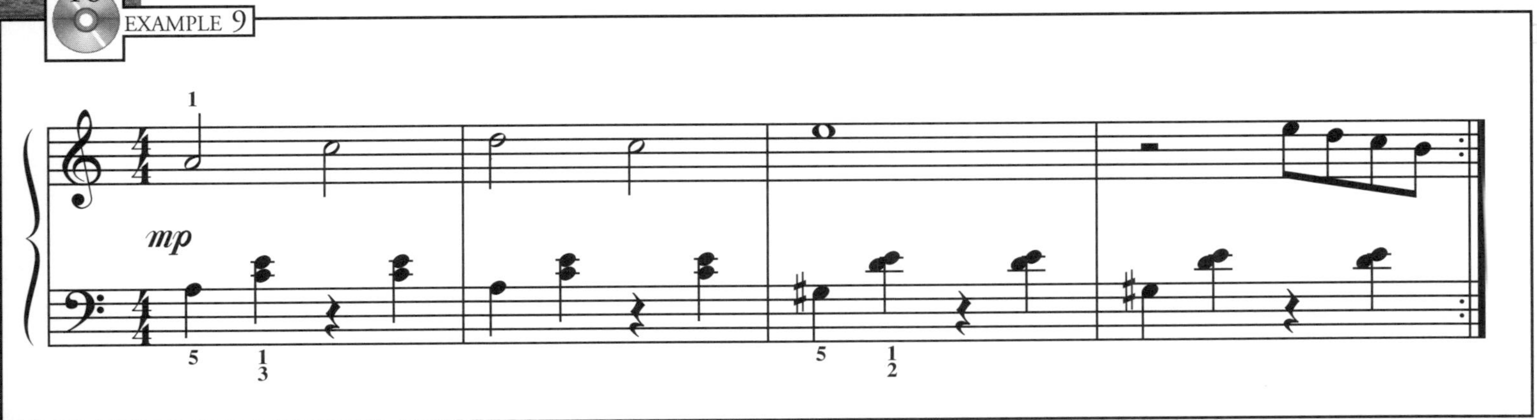

17, 18 & 19
Rasta Prophet
for Bob Marley
Bouncy reggae feel
mf
etc.
f
mp

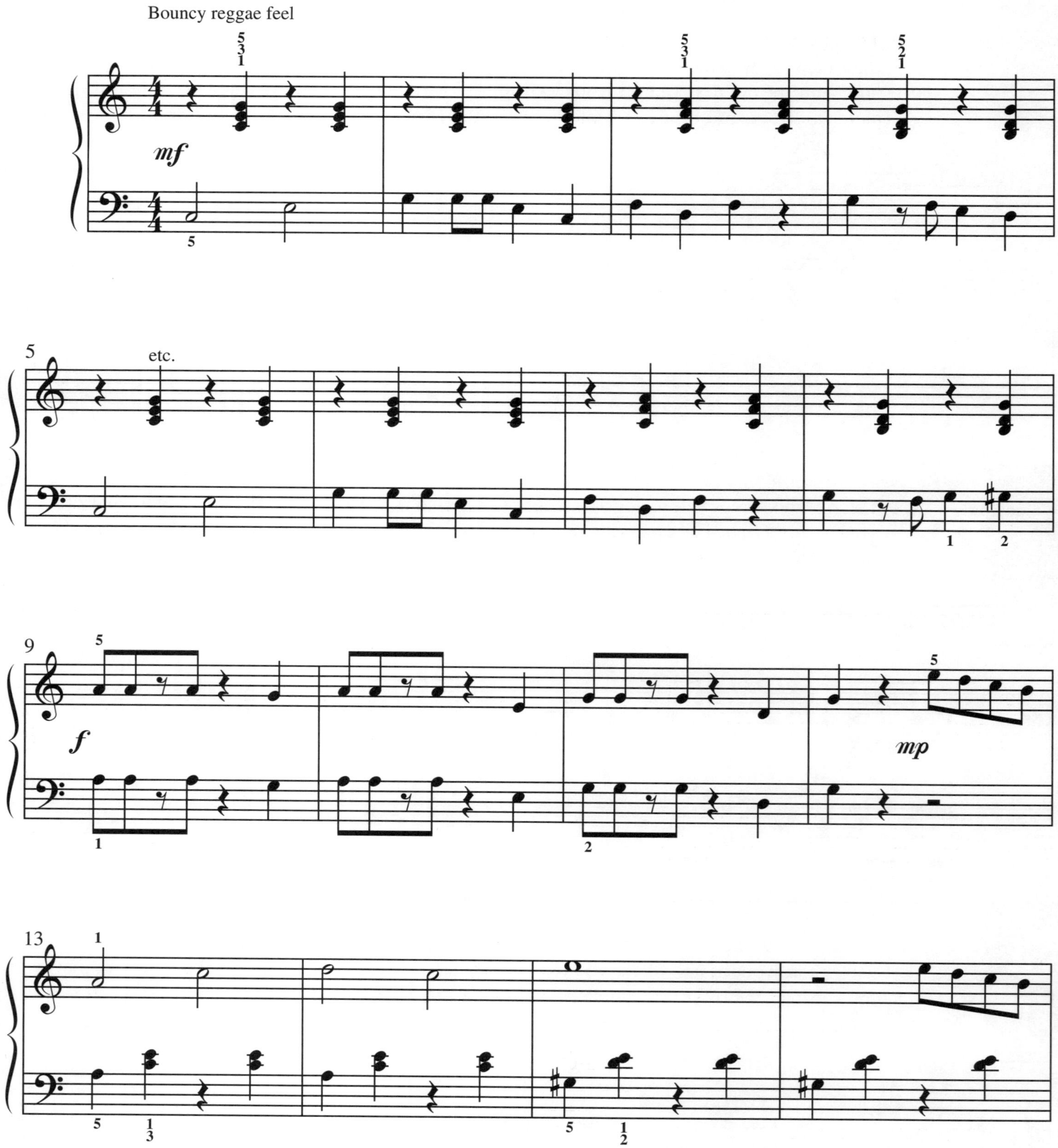

Portrait:

Mistress of Scat

For many jazz fans, the name **Ella Fitzgerald** is synonymous with jazz vocals. While she did not invent *scat singing* (a vocal style in which nonsense syllables are used to sing instrument-like passages), nobody would dispute that she was the master of the technique. A combination of technical brilliance and a unique sense of song styling made Fitzgerald's voice one of the most influential of the 20th century.

Fitzgerald grew up in a Yonkers, New York orphanage. She was discovered in her teens by bandleader and drummer Chick Webb, who not only hired her to sing, but eventually became her adoptive father. With Webb's Orchestra, Fitzgerald enjoyed her first hit in 1938 with the lighthearted *A Tisket, A Tasket*. When Webb died in 1939, a devoted Fitzgerald led his band for two years. After branching off on her own, she quickly became known for combining the effortless swing of the big-band era with the incredible virtuosity of the best bebop soloists. In 1956, Fitzgerald was signed to Verve Records and began making a series of "Songbook" recordings that spotlighted the songs of composers like Cole Porter and George Gershwin. She also recorded small-group jazz with pianist Oscar Peterson and with trumpet and vocal legend Louis Armstrong. No jazz vocalist today can escape Ella's profound influence.

ESSENTIAL LISTENING:

Top Pick: "The Complete Ella In Berlin: Mack the Knife" (1960)
> This live album, which includes tunes like *How High the Moon* and Fitzgerald's legendary version of *Mack the Knife* with "improvised" lyrics, amply testifies to the singer's creativity and complete mastery of scat.

"The Early Years, Part 2" (compilation; 1995)
> This two-disc set, which showcases Fitzgerald as she was discovering her unique style in the late 1930s and early 1940s, also includes her later recordings with Chick Webb's band.

"The Intimate Ella" (1960)
> This tender collection of duets with pianist Paul Smith demonstrates Fitzgerald's singular way with a ballad. Listeners most familiar with Fitzgerald's up-tempo work will be amazed to hear this slow, haunting music.

"Ella at Duke's Place" (1965)
> Fitzgerald teamed up with the Duke Ellington Orchestra for this fun, spirited album, which begins with ballads from the Ellington songbook before moving on to infectiously swinging numbers like *Duke's Place* and *Cottontail*.

Ella Fitzgerald *(1918–1996)*

EXERCISES

Mistress of Scat is a jazz tune with more than a hint of bebop. The melodic lines swing and lope like many of Fitzgerald's vocal lines, especially those she used when scat singing. Note that this song uses swing eighth notes. (See page 4, "Suggestions for Using This Book," for an explanation of how swing eighths work.)

For Example 10, begin by practicing one hand at a time. Make sure you are comfortable with the rhythm, especially when going from swing eighths to *triplets* (which subdivide a beat into three equal parts) and vice versa. Also note the changing roles of the hands; the right-hand melody in the first two measures is repeated in the left hand in the next two.

The keys to Example 11 are the rhythm, which uses both triplets and swing eighths, and coordination of the hands. Notice in the first two measures the way in which left-hand chords punctuate the melody, a device often used by Fitzgerald's accompanist to make the music extra tight.

Like Example 11, Example 12 relies on rhythmic precision and coordination between the hands. Note in the last phrase that you will need to use an extended position in your right hand to play the arpeggio.

23, 24 & 25
Mistress of Scat
for Ella Fitzgerald
Medium bright
Swing 8ths
mf
mp

Thumpin'

It can be easy to take the **Isley Brothers** for granted, since they seem to be part of every major development in R&B. They have constantly evolved—from a doo-wop vocal trio to a slick Motown group to a completely self-sufficient progressive R&B unit. Through each phase of their development, they have created music that is danceable, influential and immensely popular.

Vocalists O'Kelly Isley (1937–1986), Rudolph Isley (born 1939) and Ronald Isley (born 1941) began singing together in Cincinnati. The group recorded the R&B classic *Shout* in 1959, and then had a big hit with a cover of *Twist and Shout*, which in turn inspired the Beatles to record a version of their own. The Isley Brothers went on to record for Motown scoring a hit with *This Old Heart of Mine* in 1966. Feeling stifled by the label, however, the Isleys left Motown and, in 1969, formed their own label, T-Neck Records. After several more hits (including their biggest success, *It's Your Thing*), the Isleys became a six-piece band in 1969, adding younger brothers Ernie (born 1950) on guitar and Marvin (born 1953) on bass, as well as brother-in-law Chris Jasper (born 1951) on keyboards. With six talented contributors and full creative control, this incarnation of the group spent more than a decade recording albums that were both innovative and commercially successful. Led by Ronald and Ernie, the group had a hugh pop and R&B comeback hit with the 2001 album "Eternal."

ESSENTIAL LISTENING:

Top Pick: "It's Your Thing: The Story of the Isley Brothers" (compilation; 1999)
This three-disc retrospective shows off the incredible versatility and consistent quality of the Isleys' recordings.

"Greatest Hits and Rare Classics" (compilation; 1991)
While the Isleys' most creative music was yet to come, these 1960s Motown recordings are soulful and fun. In addition to the Isleys' own hits, this collection features Motown classics like *Nowhere to Run* and *I Hear a Symphony*.

"Isleys Live" (1972)
The brothers deliver the goods in abundance on this live album, which covers territory ranging from the funky unbridled passion of *Work to Do* to the somber restraint of Neil Young's *Ohio*.

"3+3" (1973)
This record introduced the younger Isleys as equal members of the band. One standout cut is the classic *That Lady*, which features psychedelic grooves and Ernie's wailing guitar.

The Isley Brothers *(formed early 1950s)*

EXERCISES

The Isley Brothers convincingly move back and forth between gentle ballads like *For the Love of You* and the driving funk of tunes like *Take Me to the Next Phase* and *That Lady*. *Thumpin'*, a medium-tempo soul tune, begins with a mellow, ballad-like introduction, then moves to the funky side of things.

Repeating the two-measure phrase in Example 13 will prepare you for playing the introduction. Play it with a gentle and lyrical feeling, but be sure not to get lazy with the rhythm.

In Example 14, the left hand should be steady and propulsive, pushing the music like the bassist in a soul band. The right hand should be crisp and precise. It's when you put the hands together that things start to get interesting, so take your time and pay attention to accuracy.

Practice Example 15 very slowly until you're comfortable with the notes and fingerings. Both hands need to be able to stretch a bit for the arpeggios, but you should be able to play these cleanly and consistently with some practice. Pay special attention to the measures in which the right hand plays alone, making sure that the rhythms are clear. Work on the grace notes in the last measure so that they sound gritty and intense; at the same time, be sure to maintain rhythmic accuracy.

29,30 & 31
Thumpin'
for the Isley Brothers
Medium tempo
mp
Funky and driving
mf
5 1 etc.

17
f
21
25
mf
etc.
29

Portrait:
Delivering the Message

I n the 1950s a style of jazz emerged called *hard bop.* Hard bop took the complex innovations of bebop and emphasized rhythmic drive and deep roots in the blues. Nobody epitomized the hard bop movement better than **Art Blakey**, known to many of his friends as "Bu" (short for Abdullah Ibn Buhaina, his Muslim name). As a drummer, Blakey's firepower was unmatched, and he brought an incredible intensity and groove to every performance. He spent more than thirty years leading the Jazz Messengers, a combo that not only created some of the best and most influential hard bop, but which also served as a sort of training school for many excellent musicians who later went on to make their own impact upon the world of jazz.

Blakey came to prominence in the mid-1940s playing with bandleaders like Fletcher Henderson, Billy Eckstine and Thelonious Monk. In the mid-1950s he and pianist Horace Silver formed the first lasting Jazz Messengers lineup. After Silver left the group, Blakey continued making innovative music and nurturing future jazz legends like saxophonists Jackie McLean, Benny Golson and Wayne Shorter, and trumpeters Lee Morgan and Freddie Hubbard. By the time of his death, dozens of jazz greats had graduated from the "Blakey Academy," and he had inspired scores of drummers.

ESSENTIAL LISTENING:

Top Pick: "Moanin'" (1958)
"Moanin'" is one of the all-time classic hard bop albums. Blakey is his usual fiery self, and trumpeter Lee Morgan, saxophonist Benny Golson and pianist Bobby Timmons turn in some of their most brilliant and passionate performances.

"Art Blakey and the Jazz Messengers" (1956)
This Columbia album showcases the early days of the Jazz Messengers, then featuring pianist/composer Horace Silver. Included are tight renditions of the Silver classics *Ecaroh* and *Nica's Dream.*

"Jazz Messengers" (1961)
This album on Impulse (not to be confused with the one above) is marked by great arrangements and impassioned playing. The Messengers burn through creative versions of standards like *I Hear a Rhapsody* and *You Don't Know What Love Is.*

"Three Blind Mice, Vol. 1" (1962)
This fabulous album demonstrates the evolving skills of musicians like Freddie Hubbard, Wayne Shorter, Curtis Fuller and Cedar Walton. Several tunes showcase individual band members, including *Blue Moon* (featuring Hubbard) and *When Lights Are Low* (featuring Fuller).

Art Blakey *(1919–1990)*

EXERCISES

In both his drumming and bandleading, Art Blakey dug in and made the music groove without being stiff or overbearing. This should be your goal as you learn *Delivering the Message*, a medium swing tune with an emphasis on the swing. Note that this song uses swing eighth notes. (See page 4, "Suggestions for Using This Book," for an explanation of how swing eighths work.)

Example 16 will help you get the feeling of the song. Let the slyly swinging rhythms be loose, but don't let that affect your precision as you learn. Be very attentive to the rhythm, taking special care to keep track of the beat—especially when you're playing syncopated lines. Note that to play the grace note in the first measure of the right-hand part, you'll slide your thumb from the G♯ down onto the A.

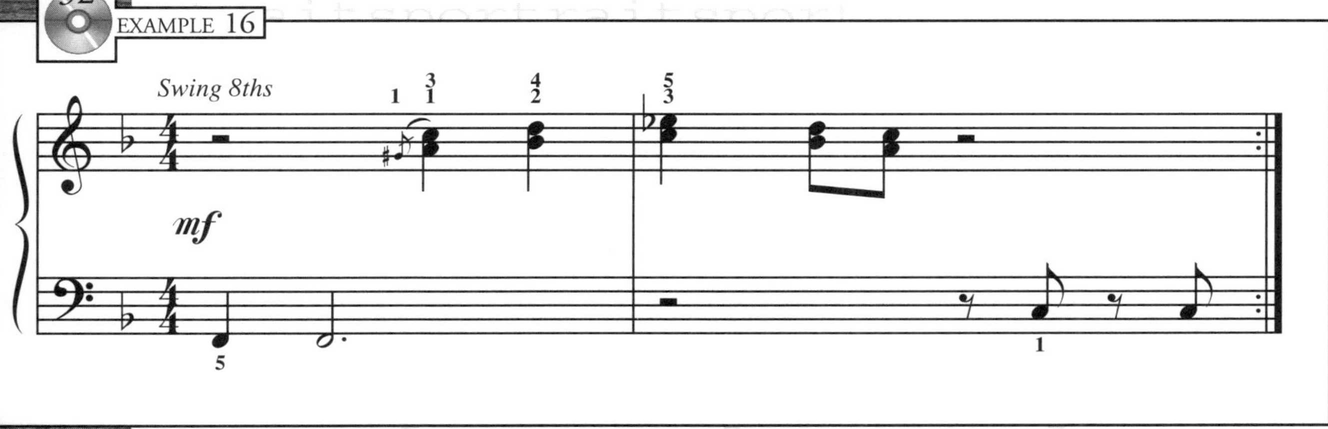

Use the same approach to rhythm and grace notes in Example 17 as you did in the previous example. Note especially the offbeat notes in the second measure. Use a metronome to ensure precision.

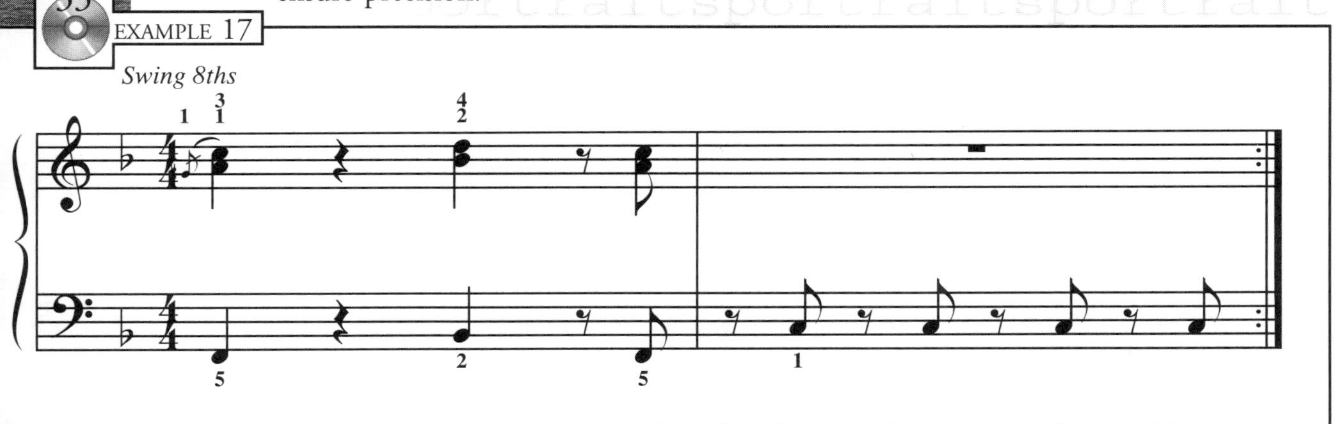

Unlike the sparse and sly examples above, Example 18 is forceful and dramatic, like the climax of a Jazz Messengers tune. In the right hand, pay particular attention to moving smoothly from one chord to the next. Put the hands together only after you can play each with the correct rhythms and without any unintentional pauses.

35, 36 & 37
Delivering the Message
for Art Blakey
Medium swing
(Swing 8ths)
mf

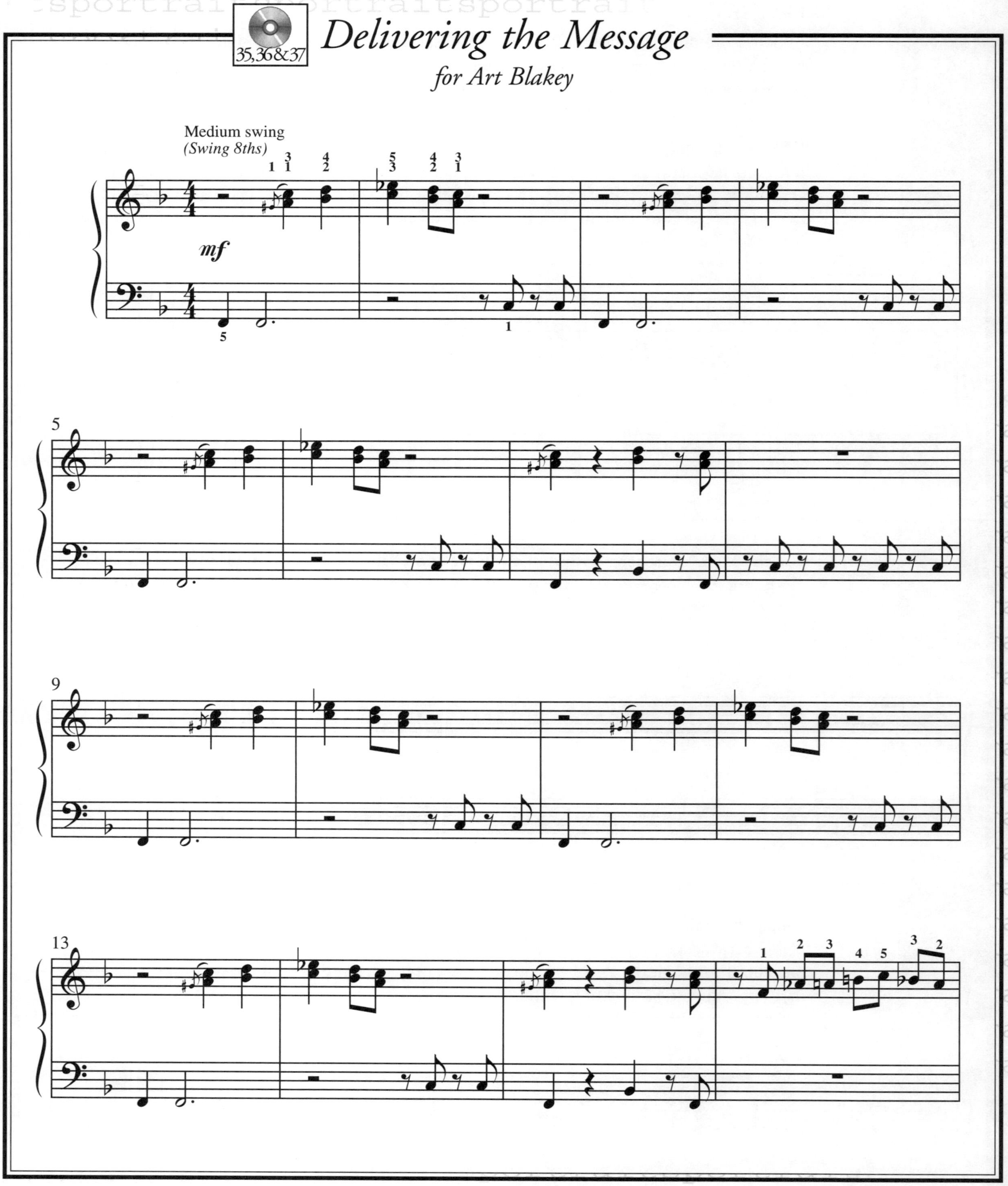

Portrait:

Cha Cha Caliente

For many years, **Tito Puente** was the most visible and respected figure in Latin music, though his popularity extended far beyond the Latin community. His incredible record of success and innovation as a bandleader led to the nickname "King of the Mambo" or simply "El Rey." He was also a master of the timbales and an accomplished player of several other instruments, including marimba and piano.

Puente grew up in a Puerto Rican family in New York. When a leg injury cut short his dreams of being a dancer, he shifted his attention to music. Puente played in several bands, including the groundbreaking Machito Orchestra. In 1947, Puente formed the Piccadilly Boys, which developed into his own band. He incorporated jazz elements into his music and, much like Art Blakey's jazz groups, Puente's bands provided important schooling for other musicians on their way to greatness, among them conga masters Ray Barretto, Willie Bobo and Mongo Santamaria. Puente's profile was boosted further in the early '70s when his song *Oye Como Va* was a huge hit for the group Santana. Puente continued to perform and record (he released more than 100 albums) until shortly before his death, often collaborating with other Latin and jazz giants.

ESSENTIAL LISTENING:

Top Pick: "Best of Tito Puente: El Rey del Timbal!" (compilation; 1997)

This Rhino anthology, which spans the years 1949–87, admirably condenses Puente's long, prolific career into a single CD. Puente's mind-blowing skills are showcased on cuts like *El Rey del Timbal* and *Tito Tombrero*.

"Cuban Carnival" (1955)

"Cuban Carnival" provides a taste of the early years of Puente's band, which included percussion masters Willie Bobo, Candido Camero, Mongo Santamaria and Carlos "Potato" Valdez.

"Dance Mania, Vol. 1" (1958)

This album, perhaps the most popular of Puente's career, will make you want to dance. The full range of salsa styles is represented throughout in tip-top performances.

"Tito Puente's Golden Latin Jazz All-Stars: In Session" (1994)

Hilton Ruiz, Mongo Santamaria, Charlie Sepulveda, Giovanni Hidalgo and Dave Valentin are among the artists who join Puente on this disc, which features burning instrumental solos.

Tito Puente *(1923–2000)*

EXAMPLES

Cha Cha Caliente is a medium-tempo tune that draws upon Latin styles like *cha-cha* (a rhythmic dance) and *son montuno* (montuno: a type of repeated phrase used in salsa music). Here, you'll get your feet wet with some of the techniques that Puente and the members of his band used in creating their classic music.

Example 19 depends on controlled use of syncopation in a cha-cha pattern. In the first two measures, the right hand plays on the "and" of each beat (counting "one-*and*-two-*and*-three-*and*-four-*and*"). The next two measures combine this with additional notes in the right hand. Try using a metronome with this exercise, and make sure that you feel comfortable with the rhythm before moving on.

Example 20 also makes use of syncopation in the right hand, this time in the style of a montuno. In order to get the notes and rests to fall in the right places, try charting or graphing the rhythm visually, analyzing it before you play and counting aloud while you play.

Example 21, used as a section ending in the piece, is rhythmically simpler than Examples 19 and 20. Make sure you get the fingering down smoothly and can play the phrase without hesitation.

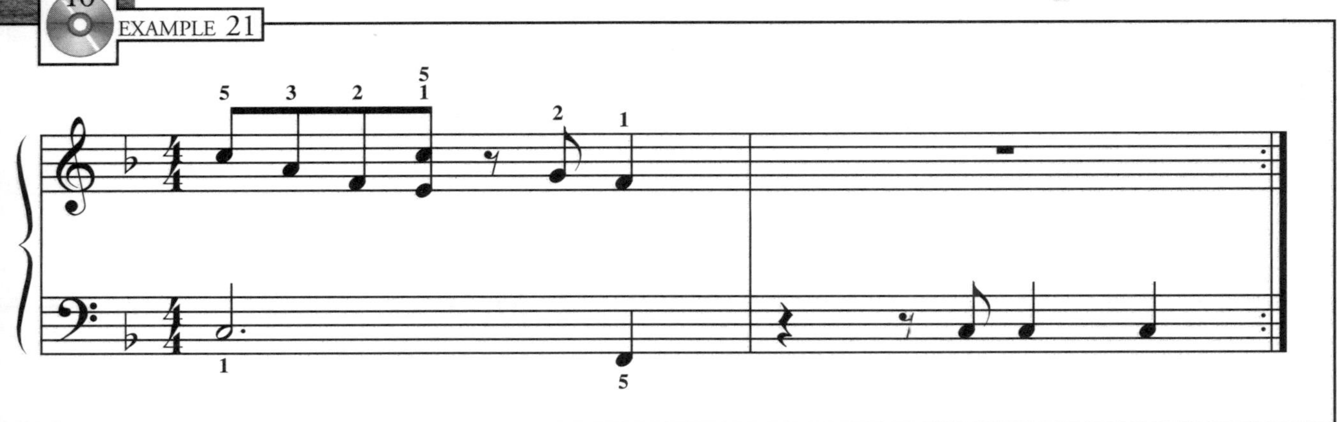

Cha Cha Caliente

for Tito Puente

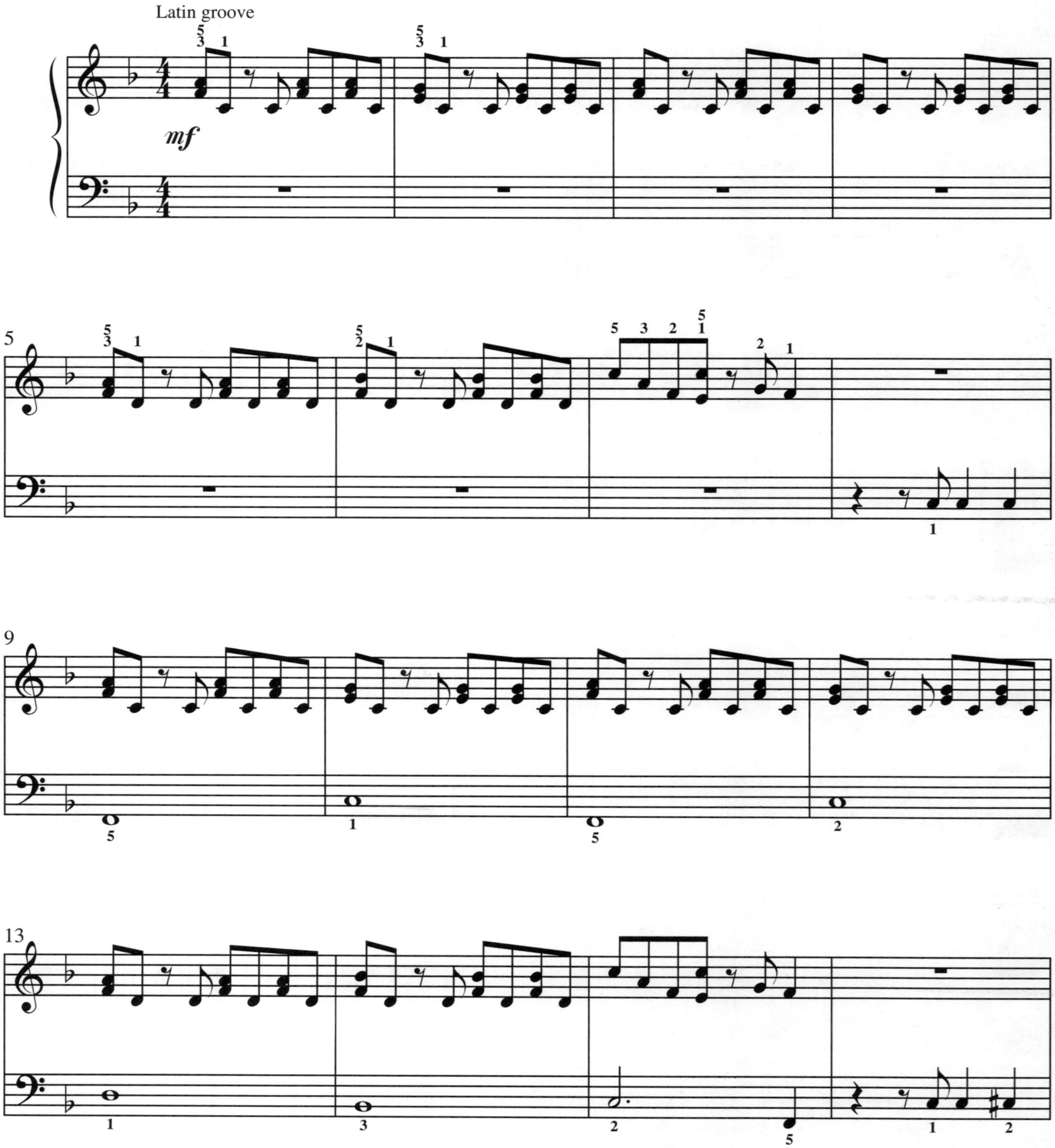

Shades of Blue

Whenever you hear a modern electric guitarist playing the blues, you are probably hearing the influence of **T-Bone Walker**. While there were great blues guitarists before him, Walker was the first major blues artist to make use of the electric guitar and its capacity for single-note solos and lead lines. His influence can be heard in guitarists ranging from B. B. King to Chuck Berry to Stevie Ray Vaughan. He left behind a rich legacy of his own recordings, which also showcase his excellent singing and songwriting.

Born Aaron Thibeaux Walker (his middle name was the basis for "T-Bone"), Walker grew up in Texas. At age ten he became the "lead boy" for Blind Lemon Jefferson, leading the sightless blues legend from place to place. Walker played in various bands, eventually joining Les Hite's Band in 1939. He soon put together his own band and began showing off his amplified lead lines and onstage acrobatics like splits and playing the guitar behind his back. Walker's recording career took off in 1947 with *Call It Stormy Monday,* one of the most popular and frequently covered blues songs ever. Walker began a struggle with ulcers in the 1950s that continued until his death, but he continued to play concerts and festivals throughout the USA and Europe.

ESSENTIAL LISTENING:

Top Pick: "Blues Masters: The Very Best of T-Bone Walker" (compilation; 2000)
This Rhino collection brings together some of the music that forever changed the way the blues are played. No blues fan should be without Walker's recording of *Stormy Monday.*

"The Complete Imperial Recordings" (compilation; 1991)
This two-disc set of recordings from 1950–54 is strong and entertaining throughout. Walker had established himself by this point, so what you hear is a confident blues genius burning through some of his best songs.

"T-Bone Blues" (1959)
Walker recorded these songs for Atlantic in 1955–57. His phenomenal guitar playing is here outstandingly showcased in a number of instrumentals, most notably the multi-guitarist "duel" on *Two Bones and a Pick.*

"I Want A Little Girl" (1967)
Recorded live at a Paris concert, this album shows an older Walker to still be a performer of depth, subtlety and greatness.

T-Bone Walker *(1910–1973)*

EXERCISES

Shades of Blue is a laid-back, medium-tempo blues tune with a feeling that evokes T-Bone Walker classics like *Vida Lee* and *Call It Stormy Monday*. In addition, the *fills* (melodic phrases that fill in pauses in the main melody) in the right hand hint at the types of guitar licks that Walker played between vocal phrases.

Many of T-Bone's guitar licks alternate triplet and sixteenth-note rhythms. Example 22 will prepare you to make those transitions. Use a metronome to make sure that the beat is steady and the rhythms are precise when you make these switches.

Example 23 will prepare you for the introduction and the ending. Play these rich-sounding chords cleanly and with a steady groove.

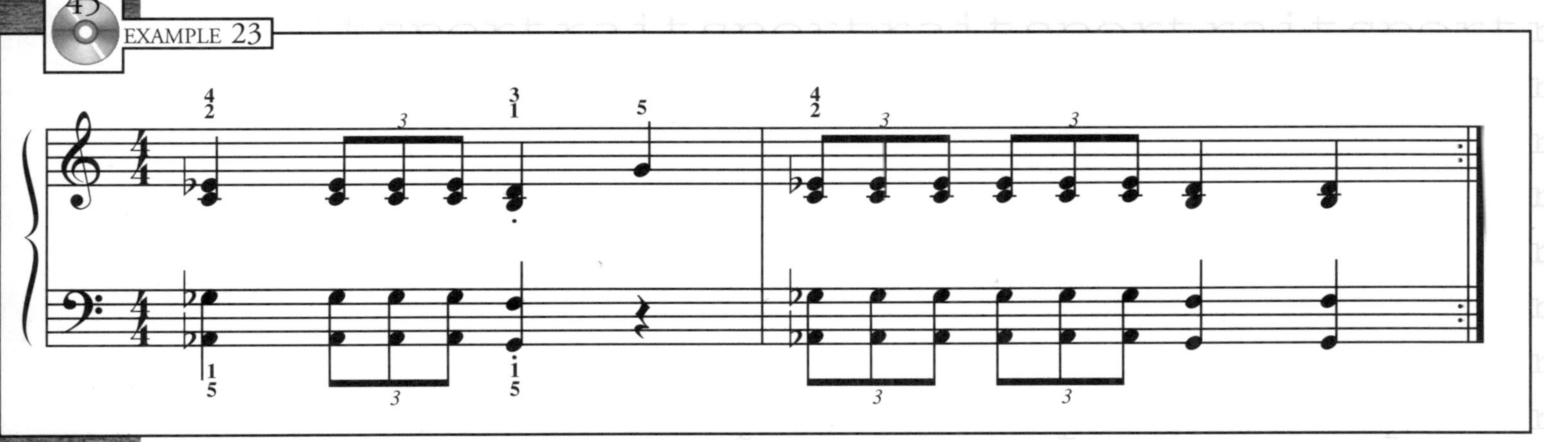

Example 24 will prepare you for a few of the devices you'll encounter in *Shades of Blue*. The first two measures use chords in the right hand over a *walking bass* (an active bass line that uses mainly quarter notes) in the left hand. The roles of the hands switch in the next two measures as the right hand plays a guitar-style fill. Note that you'll need to switch from sixteenth notes to triplets while maintaining a steady beat.

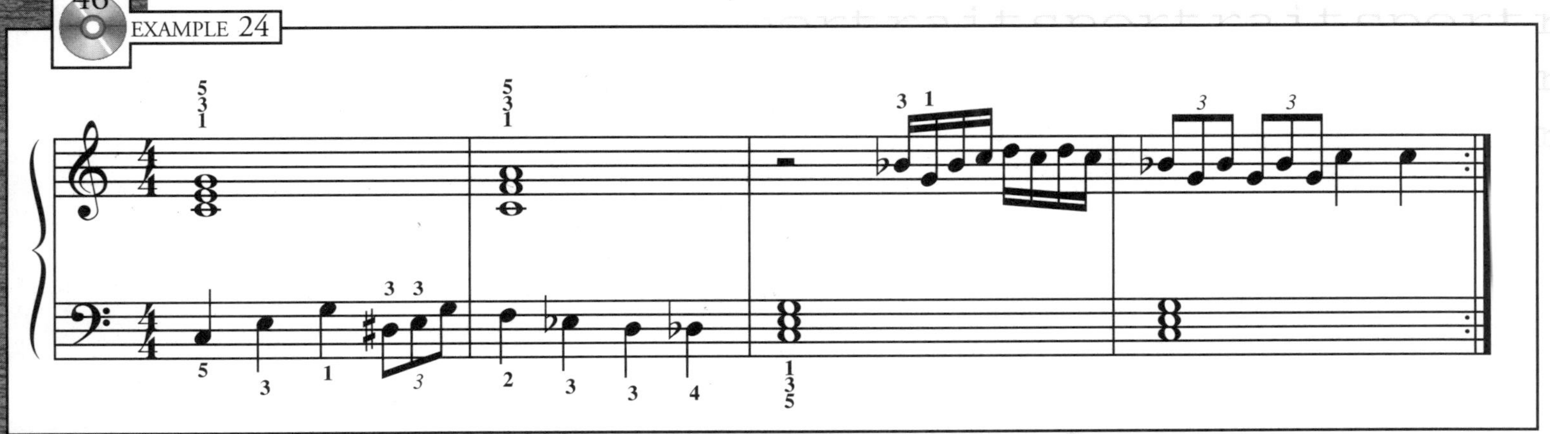

47, 48 & 49
Shades of Blue
for T-Bone Walker
Laid-back blues feel
f
mf
Portrait: Shades of Blue

f
Portraits: Book 2

Roots Rockin'

The **Rolling Stones** have billed themselves as the "World's Greatest Rock Band," and it is hard to argue with that claim. Unlike many of their contemporaries in the 1960s (such as the Beatles), the Rolling Stones drew on Chicago blues to create a gritty, hard-driving sound. To many people, the essence of rock 'n' roll can be found in the passionate vocals of Mick Jagger (born 1943), the grungy guitar of Keith Richards (born 1941) and the solid rhythm of drummer Charlie Watts (born 1941) and bassist Bill Wyman (born 1936). Few songwriters can match the output of Richards and Jagger.

The Rolling Stones, who took their name from a song by Muddy Waters, played their first gig in 1962. A year later they made their first recordings and soon began making the charts, first in Britain, then in the United States. At first they recorded blues, soul and rock cover songs, but before long, their own songs found massive success. Their first of many No. 1 hits in the USA came with the classic *Satisfaction* in 1965. The "bad boy" image and lifestyle developed by some of the band's members caused turmoil, but the Rolling Stones' musical output remained consistent for decades. By the 1990s, they had amassed dozens of hit singles and albums and were one of the most successful live acts in the world.

ESSENTIAL LISTENING:

Top Pick: "Exile On Main Street" (1972)
This is the Stones in a nutshell: passionate singing, gritty guitar, groovin' drums and terrific songs. *Tumbling Dice* is just one of the songs that demonstrates how well the Stones developed their unique take on Southern soul.

"Out of Our Heads" (1965)
This album shows the Stones in transition—playing classic soul tunes as only they could, but also coming into their own with originals like *Satisfaction*.

"Let It Bleed" (1969)
The Stones' response to the Beatles' "Let It Be," this raw album is full of great performances of tunes that have become classics, including *Gimme Shelter* and *You Can't Always Get What You Want*.

"Jump Back: The Best of The Rolling Stones, 1971–1993"
While most people consider the 1960s to be the Stones' most fertile period, this two-disc compilation demonstrates their creative vitality in the following decades in cuts like *Angie, Wild Horses* and *Waiting on a Friend*.

The Rolling Stones *(formed 1962)*

PHOTO • CHUCK PULIN/ COURTESY OF STAR FILE PHOTO, INC.

EXERCISES

From *Under My Thumb* to *Jumpin' Jack Flash* to *Start Me Up,* the Rolling Stones have been a wellspring of classic medium-tempo tunes that are rock solid but not too busy. *Roots Rockin'* rocks and rolls along in the same spirit.

The left hand in Example 25 should be solid and rhythmically precise, while the right hand should move seamlessly from each chord or note to the next. Once you've accomplished this, work on coordinating the hands. The result is a phrase that combines a Bill Wyman-style bass with a chordal riff in the style of Keith Richards.

Example 26 also combines a chordal riff with a bass line, but in a much more intense and varied way. Note the *anticipations*—in this case, places where a new chord lands half a beat before the beginning of the next measure.

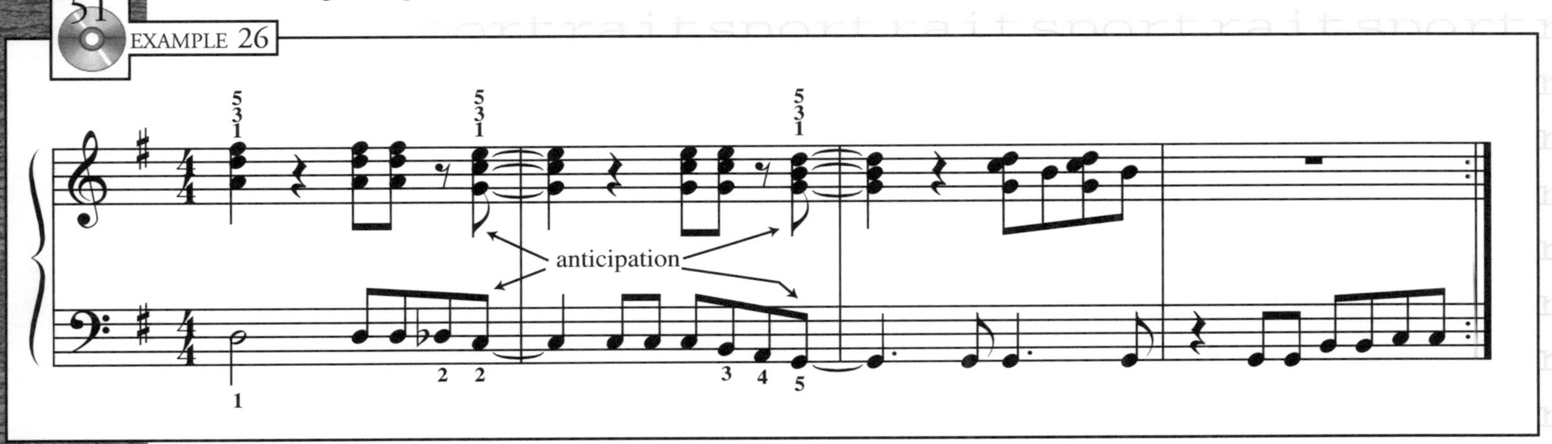

Example 27, especially the last two measures of the right hand, hints at the sort of blues phrase that often creeps into the Stones' music.

53,54&55
Roots Rockin'
for the Rolling Stones
Medium rock groove
mf

17
f
21
25
29
Portraits: Book 2 | 41

Portrait:

Red-Hot Rag

There are few figures in jazz more puzzling than **Jelly Roll Morton**. There is no denying that Morton had a great impact on jazz. To this day, however, he is dogged by his infamous insistence that he invented jazz in 1902. While few people take this claim seriously, it should not obscure the fact that as a bandleader, arranger and composer he was brilliant and influential, helping to shape the development and sound of jazz bands.

Morton was born Ferdinand Lamothe in New Orleans, where he was exposed to a broad range of music from Western classical music to ragtime and the blues. While it was not as clean or "sophisticated" as the styles of the top pianists in New York, Morton developed a wonderful and rhythmically exciting piano style from his various influences. In the mid-1920s, he moved to Chicago and made some crucial early jazz records with his group, the Red Hot Peppers; these songs featured memorable rhythms and melodies and tremendous variety throughout. Through most of the 1930s, Morton did not record, though Benny Goodman had great success with Morton's *King Porter Stomp*. Late in the decade, Morton was recorded for the Library of Congress, playing the piano, singing and talking about his life.

ESSENTIAL LISTENING:

Top Pick: "Greatest Hits" (compilation; 1996)
If you own only one Jelly Roll Morton recording, it should be this excellent RCA compilation. Tracks like *The Pearls* and *Black Bottom Stomp* show early jazz at its most innovative and irresistible.

"Blues & Stomps From Rare Piano Rolls"
(recorded 1924–26)
These piano rolls made by Morton showcase the musician's inimitable keyboard style. Among the tunes included are *Grandpa's Spells, King Porter Stomp* and *Dead Man Blues*.

"Morton Centennial: His Complete Victor Recordings"
(recorded 1926–39)
Can't get enough Jelly Roll? Move on to this five-disc set, which features multiple takes of Morton classics as well as great playing from sidemen like clarinetist Omer Simeon and banjoist Johnny St. Cyr.

"The Library of Congress Recordings, Volume 1" (1938)
On this first CD from a storehouse of late recordings on which Morton both plays and talks, the pianist proves himself to be an articulate and fascinating storyteller as well as a consummate, energetic musician.

Jelly Roll Morton *(1890–1941)*

EXERCISES

Many Jelly Roll Morton tunes, such as *The Pearls* and *King Porter Stomp,* fall into the cracks between ragtime and jazz: The extended forms are much like those of ragtime, but they swing like jazz. *Sweet Jelly* is a medium-bright tempo tune of a similar dual character. Note that this song uses swing eighth notes. (See page 4, "Suggestions for Using This Book," for an explanation of how swing eighths work.)

Example 28 is useful in developing the coordination you'll need to play *Sweet Jelly*. The left hand plays in a style called *stride,* in which an "oom-pah" feeling is created by playing a bass note followed by a chord, while the right hand plays a swinging melody. Make sure your playing is accurate and rock-steady before moving on.

Because of the highly sectional nature of his tunes, Morton often used transitional phrases to move from one section to the next. Different versions of the phrase in Example 29 are used in a similar manner in *Sweet Jelly*. Pay particular attention to fingerings; in several places, the same finger slides down from a black key to a white key.

Example 30 takes you through two variations on a phrase from *Sweet Jelly*. The first two measures have a sly, subtle feeling, while the last two measures are more brash and dramatic. Work on emphasizing the contrast between these sections, and make them swing.

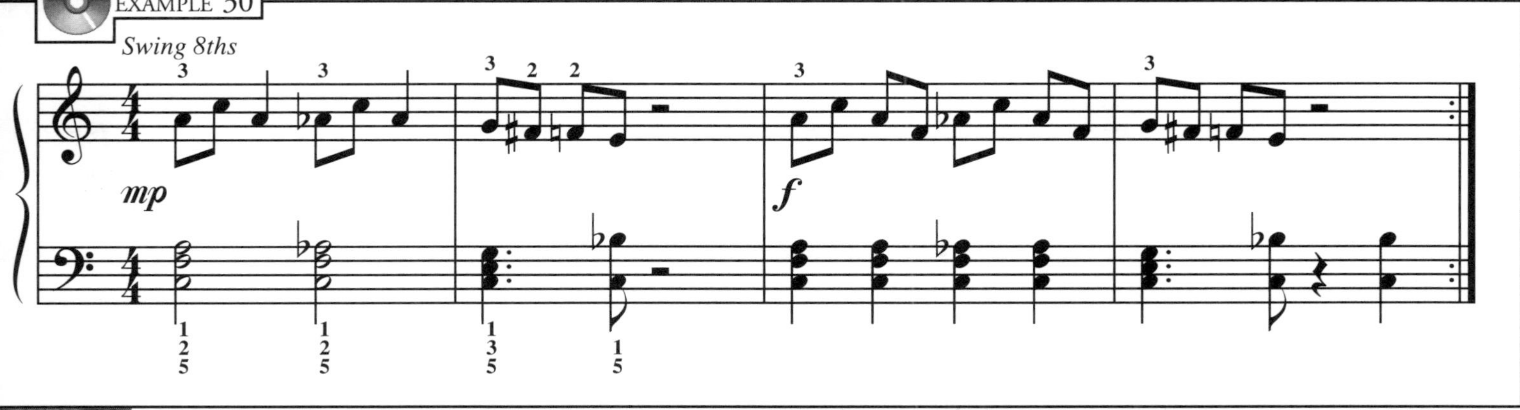

59, 60 & 61
Red-Hot Rag
for Jelly Roll Morton
Medium bright
Swing 8ths
mp
mf

33
mp
37
41
mf
f
45